MW00626770

MOURNING
Light

DISCOVERING HOPE, JOY, & PEACE
AFTER THE PASSING OF A LOVED ONE

DAMITA BRAYE-GONZALEZ,
LPC/ LMFT

HIGH BRIDGE BOOKS
HOUSTON

Mourning Light
By Damita Braye-Gonzalez

Copyright © 2016 by Damita Braye-Gonzalez
All rights reserved.

Printed in the United States of America
ISBN (Paperback): 978-1-940024-91-2
ISBN (eBook): 978-1-940024-92-9

All rights reserved. Except in the case of brief quotations embodied in critical articles and reviews, no portion of this book may be reproduced, stored in a retrieval system, or transmitted in any form or by any means—electronic, mechanical, photocopy, recording, scanning, or other—without the prior written permission from the author.

High Bridge Books titles may be purchased in bulk for educational, business, fundraising, or sales promotional use. For information please contact High Bridge Books via www.HighBridgeBooks.com/contact.

Unless otherwise indicated, all Scripture quotations are taken from the Holy Bible, New Living Translation (NLT), copyright © 1996, 2004, 2007 by Tyndale House Foundation. Used by permission of Tyndale House Publishers, Inc., Carol Stream, Illinois 60188. All rights reserved.

Published in Houston, Texas by High Bridge Books

DEDICATION

Mom, this one is for you, with all my love, forever! This book is dedicated to my best friend, my mother! There are not enough words to give you the tribute that you are worthy of. You have been the greatest example of a mother that a girl could have. I am so blessed to have had the opportunity and memories over the years that will forever be cherished and hold a special place in my heart. Thank you for being an amazing mother and an example for me to live by. The woman, the mother, and the wife that I am today is all because of you. You were my angel here on earth and now my angel from heaven, always watching over me.

CONTENTS

ACKNOWLEDGEMENTS

My husband, Domingo Gonzalez, you are my anchor that keeps me grounded no matter what comes my way! I am always safe and protected with you. I thank God each and every day for you being in my life. You are indeed my soul mate, and I love you with all my heart. Heaven sent you just for me.

My children, Damia Le'Cara and Domingo Leandre'... You are my greatest reward and true blessings from Heaven above. You indeed were your grandmother's heart.

Dad, you have been my teacher and guide, and I thank you for being a great example of a father and a protector. I love you!

Demarco Henderson, thank you for always being available—no matter how far away—to talk with me, advise me spiritually, and pray for me continuously. And thank you for encouraging me to write this book.

Pastor Eric Majette and First Lady Vonda, thank you for allowing my mother to have a platform and support for her God-given gifts to be recognized and utilized. I am so grateful for the love, opportunity, and confidence you have extended to her. On behalf of me and my family, we are forever grateful.

Marilyn Harvey, my cousin from birth and sister for life, thank you for always being there when it counts. I love you. I know that, because of your friendship, I am never alone.

Aunt Olivia, Uncle Steve Foreman, and Richmond family… thank you for standing close and taking the meaning of *family* to another level. Your love and prayers have played a vital role in my recovery. I love you all.

Lastly, a special thanks to Mrs. Sylvia Freeman and Sheri Fayton who were incredibly supportive and took me in as "family" and played a vital role in my recovery. You were there every day and every step of the way, and I am forever grateful.

Aunt Dot, thank you for stepping in and playing a vital role. My love for you is endless.

There is no way to list and thank everyone who has been a true blessing in my life on this journey, but to my friends and family, thank you so much. Know that your love has helped me to endure this difficult and painful time in my life. I am forever grateful.

INTRODUCTION

This book is for those who have lost a loved one and have wondered, "Where do I go from here? How will I get there? Do I have the strength to get through this?" I have asked myself those same questions. When you experience losing a loved one, you may feel like you have been punched in your stomach and can't catch your breath. It may feel like some type of out-of-body experience in which you see the people and are aware of what's going on around you, but you are not connected to any of it. If neither of those have been your experience, then perhaps you have felt faint or simply numb. Nevertheless, the experience is like nothing you have experienced before.

The first few days can truly feel like a blur, as if you are hovering around on a cloud in slow motion, zipping in and out of the reality of what happened. At times, the fog gets thick, and you can't think or feel. You simply feel blank.

People seem to come around immediately as the news spreads, and suddenly, you can't keep up with the people calling, coming, and going. Decisions and arrangements have to be made, and usually, you have only a week to do it. You just want to stop the madness, check out, and scream. But there is no time for that. People are counting on you, and things have to get done.

By the time you are reading this book, you have probably gone through this experience. You may have accomplished the task of finalizing the funeral arrangements and are trying to figure out what's next. Your journey has begun. The hardest part after the funeral service is when everyone leaves, and suddenly, the flood of reality surfaces. It becomes difficult to put off your thoughts and feelings any longer. This can be an overwhelming time and also a time when depression can set in.

During these moments, your get-up-and-go may have got up and left you without any motivation. You most likely won't want to get up, get out, push yourself, and allow others to join you on this journey.

You may want to prevent people from telling you how to feel, what to feel, and how long to feel certain ways. They mean well but don't always know the most comforting or helpful things to say. They can have a tendency to make you feel confused or angry, so be willing to set boundaries.

Additionally, you may have those who offer cliché statements like "be strong" and "don't cry." Who is that really for? To cry is a normal reaction to pain, and it is not a sign of weakness. So feel what you feel; it does a heart good. Grief affects your heart. It is not something that you necessarily can understand or control through logic.

You probably realize that people don't know how to comfort you. Interestingly enough, I have

seen those who are mourning turn around and comfort those who are there to support them.

At times, you will need alone time. Time alone provides moments to process your feelings and work toward healing. Don't avoid what you feel; embrace your feelings. You may feel uncomfortable, or you may experience fear in facing feelings that you think will overwhelm you, but you can make it through.

Each day will be an experience that you have not encountered previously, but with God's grace, He will see you though on the journey.

1

GRIEF

Grief is a normal and internal feeling one experiences in response to a loss. Grief is painful and can affect you physically and emotionally as you adjust to the pain of losing someone you love. It is an unexpected, unbelievable, shocking surge of emotions that you feel physically but can't always explain. Sometimes, the emotional surge can be so intense that you feel as if you have momentarily lost consciousness, are moving in slow motion, or are simply disconnected. This emotionally painful experience is necessary for healing. It is not possible to get back to normal and move forward without the process of grieving; it is unavoidable.

Grief is internal and relates to the thoughts and feelings regarding the loss and can include shock, confusion, denial, anger, sadness, rage, depression, isolation, and more.

The process of grieving allows time to collect your thoughts and grasp the reality of the situation. Because of this, it is important to give yourself permission and patience. Although we may never completely stop experiencing our loss, in time, the frequency and intensity of our emotions will decrease.

Bereavement is a period after a loss during which grief is experienced and mourning occurs. Grief is the beginning of mourning. Mourning is the outward expression of the loss, and it is means to adapt and make changes. Mourning can be a valuable time to reflect, experience memories, deepen and appreciate your love, and heal from the inside out. You can't heal what you don't allow yourself to feel. Mourning can represent isolation, withdrawal, disconnection, and a discontinuance of something.

Although we can grieve on other levels—such as from a divorce, children leaving home, job loss, lack of job promotion, miscarriage, or loss of health—loss is not just considered from the perspective of death. In this book, we will be addressing grief regarding the loss of a loved one, a physical death.

In sharing my own journey through grief, you will hear the stages of grief that I have travelled through, which have been labeled by Elisabeth Kübler-Ross. In 1969, she published *On Death and Dying*, and her model has been adopted widely since that time. According to Kübler-Ross, the stages of grief are as follows:

- **Denial**: disbelief, "it can't be true"
- **Anger**: intense emotions of frustration
- **Bargaining**: negotiating for extended life
- **Depression**: incredible periods of sadness/despair

- **Acceptance**: coming to terms with the loss

3

SYMPTOMS OF GRIEF

For a period of time during grief, it is normal to experience any of the symptoms listed below. It is the prolonged episodes that are a concern and can lead to more problematic issues. If you experience these symptoms for more than six months, you should seek counseling from someone who has experience in grief therapy.

EMOTIONAL SYMPTOMS

- Guilt
- Anger
- Bitterness
- Consumed in thought regarding the loss
- Emotionally numb
- Disconnected

- Irritability
- Sadness
- Depression
- Restricted emotionally and with affect
- Worry/anxiety
- Guilt
- Loneliness
- Feeling of abandonment

PHYSICAL SYMPTOMS

- Headaches
- Pain throughout body
- Chest pain
- Digestion difficulties
- Fatigue
- Decreased appetite
- Insomnia
- Crying
- Depersonalization
- Nausea
- Abdominal issues

SOCIAL SYMPTOMS

- Detached from others
- Isolation of yourself
- Withdrawn
- Avoidant
- Lack of motivation
- Overly sensitive
- Dependent

SPIRITUAL SYMPTOMS

- Questioning your belief in God
- Spiritual avoidance
- Anger toward God
- Spiritual confusion

BEHAVIORAL SYMPTOMS

- Difficulty concentrating
- Forgetfulness
- Needing to talk about the loss of a loved one

- Retelling the story of a loved one's death
- Scattered thoughts

4

HELP

O n this journey, these are some things that you may consider or encounter in acquiring the support and help of others.

First, grief can leave you feeling so alone, but it isn't something that you should attempt to handle on your own. You may be unable to make reasonable decisions at such a stressful time. Your ability to care adequately for yourself may go unmanaged, and you may not realize the essential things you need such as rest and balanced meals. Allow others to be there for you to help see you through.

Second, people who come to help following the loss of a loved one don't always know the ways they can be of help other than bringing food over, sitting with you, and getting whatever you need. So during the grieving process, you may have to help people help you by communicating what you need so they can best accommodate you during your time of bereavement.

Third, you may discover the challenges people have during this delicate time by their responses to your crying. They may attempt to rush you through it or say, "Don't cry," "Be strong," "You will be okay," or "God knows best, and He doesn't make mistakes." Statements like these are well-intended, but they can communicate to a grieving person that it is wrong to grieve. Feeling sad and frightened is a normal reaction to grief.

Fourth, if you seem to be holding up, it can appear as if you are handling it well, are okay, and are "being strong." As a result, others may think you don't need help and that you've got it under control.

Fifth, there is a side to grief where you may feel okay but feel guilty for not appearing to be mourning. Remember that you don't have to meet anyone's expectations regarding your grief, and you may have good days and bad days.

As you see, fulfilling the expectations of others while you grieve can become complicated, causing you to become unsure of what's right and wrong. Professionals can help you to exercise what you are feeling so that you can work through your grief.

Help is always available to resolve concerns and difficult challenges that you face in life. If you encounter periods of your journey when you feel stuck or lost, seek help. During chronic periods of grief, there may be a lack of motivation—emotionally, socially, or physically. Life may appear empty or meaningless, and there may be an intense longing for your loved one. Extreme avoidance, anger, and bitterness make everyday living a challenge. Seek help to restore your hope and become encouraged to continue with life and relationships.

5

RECAP OF THE LAST DAY

I will never forget what happened on July 5, 2014, and I would have never thought it would be the very last time I would see my mother. She was full of life that day and was happy to be celebrating the belated Fourth of July as our festivities had been postponed due to rain on the previous day. She was insistent about celebrating the Fourth of July. "If not the fourth… then, the fifth," she said.

She always liked to entertain, and she enjoyed people and celebrating. She was serving many that day. She would eat and talk in between serving the guests, but was mainly focused on serving them. For those who knew her, she was always eager to share something that she had read, dreamed about, or received in prayer.

On the fifth, she shared her latest revelation to those who were drawn to her discussion about the cross of Jesus. She felt that God was revealing to her the meaning of the cross at a deeper level. People were intrigued with what she shared and were listening attentively. Periodically, she would stop to have dessert or make another plate for a guest who had just arrived. She was truly a servant of the Lord and to her family and friends.

One of the last friends she served that day was her friend of many years, Sylvia. Sylvia indicated that she really felt moved to gather that day, to have some time to talk and share with her friend, my mom. They both had worked together over the years in nursing at various hospitals and other facilities. They were two extremely busy people, so they were not able to get together as often as they would have liked. But when they did, it didn't take them long to catch up and feel like they hadn't missed a beat.

As it became later in the evening, people were asking, "Where is Clara?" Some said they thought she went inside or upstairs, and others said, "She was just standing right there and suddenly disappeared." After looking and no luck, I began to ask the same question, so I called her on her cell phone. She answered, and I asked, "Mom, where are you?"

In a sweet voice, she replied, "At home."

I said, "Mom, we are having a celebration. What are you doing home?"

She indicated she went home to take her medicine because she felt a little indigestion. She said she had taken her medicine and felt better. She then told me, "I will see you at church tomorrow." We briefly talked about what a wonderful evening we had, and I told her I couldn't have done it without her.

Later that night, she talked with the pastor's wife, Vonda, in preparation for Sunday.

I would have never in a million years thought I would never see or talk to my mom again. You suddenly think, *If only I would have known that would be my last day with my loved one…* You tell yourself what you would have said or done differently. It is normal for these thoughts to cross your mind as you try to process what happened.

Since then, my life has forever changed. I am not the same.

In your mind and out loud, you repeat the last hours, moments, and minutes over and over again to try to digest emotionally and accept what has happened. It is normal to do so and may happen for some time until you are able to process the loss. Take as much time that is needed to grieve, but just grieve over your loss and loved one. Sometimes, you may need a grief counselor to talk with and to help with processing your loss. Such counselors can be beneficial for helping you to get back on a road of recovery.

LESSONS IN LIFE

1. Each day is special. Make each day count, and cherish every moment with those you love. Live each day as if it were your last.

2. Honor your loved ones here on Earth and away in Heaven.

3. In *Today Matters*, John Maxwell said, "Today matters. Yesterday happened last night, tomorrow has not come, today is all we have, and today matters! Make today count."

MAKE TODAY MATTER

Take some time to remember your last conversation and your final moments together with your loved one. As you take time to reflect, what would you have liked to say? A lot of times, people wish they could say just one more thing, one more time.

Right now, take this time to say it out loud. Free yourself from the emotional burden of what you cannot say because your loved one is no longer with you. Your loved one will always be with you in spirit. Take the time to express what you want to say.

6

MY JOURNEY BEGINS

Early the next morning, at about 5:30 a.m., my father attempted to contact me, but I did not hear the call. He proceeded to call my daughter who slept in the next room, informing her that her grandmother, my mom, was having distress and that the ambulance was en route to get her. Immediately, she ran into my room and said, "Dada is taking Mama C to the hospital."

I jumped up and began to put on my clothes. I called to verify the message with my dad, and he stated, "Your mother is having difficulty breathing. The ambulance came, and we're en route to the hospital."

I told him I would be right there. Although it took only minutes, it felt like an eternity. I couldn't get there fast enough.

We arrived at the hospital in what seemed like minutes, and I found my dad on the floor in a private room crying. I walked into the waiting room and said, "Dad!"

He turned around. With tears running down his face, he said, "It doesn't look good. They're working on her."

Suddenly, I was afraid. That was the moment when the Earth shook for me. I frantically went down the hall to find my mother and someone who could tell me what was going on. I wanted to be by her side, to see her, and to let her know she was going to be okay.

As I walked down the hallway to find the doctors and see my mom, a nurse pointed me to a closed-off room. I slid back the glass door and found them working on my mom. What I saw was an unforgettable scene as my mother was laying there with someone on top of her, physically doing CPR, and a team of others was aggressively providing treatment. A nurse told me that I should not be in there and asked me to leave until they could come to get me.

At that moment, I stood in shock and thought, *Oh, God! This is serious! Oh, God!* As I somehow made it down the corridor back to my dad, I sat in the chair with tears rolling down my face. I was in shock about what was happening. It was surreal. I couldn't pray. I couldn't talk. I just sat there in sheer shock. My family was sitting around, quiet and in a daze.

Moments later, the doctor came in to give us discouraging details and inquired if we wanted them to continue working on her. She seemed to be asking a question but yet making a statement.

I asked, "Are you asking us or telling us?"

She stated that they had done all they could, and if it were her mother, she wouldn't want the doctors to continue working on her. It had been at least an hour, but there was still no heartbeat.

My father pleaded with the doctor, saying, "My wife is my best friend. Do all you can to save her. I can take care of her. Do anything you can to save her."

At that point, the emergency room doctor allowed us to return to the room where they were working on her because she needed us to see that they had exhausted all options. I wished she hadn't because that was the most traumatizing thing that I have ever seen. I turned my head because I couldn't watch anymore. With one last glimpse to see if this was really happening, my mom's body repeatedly being shocked, I said, "Dad, stop it. That's enough."

He held on a minute and said, "Okay. Stop."

At that moment, they stopped and began to disconnect her. They told us we could take our time and spend as long as we wanted with her. Everyone was crying. Dad was draped over her on one side, pleading for her not to leave him. My son was standing behind him and holding on to him in dismay. On the other side, my daughter was on her knees, holding on to my mom and calling her name over and over. I stood behind her, frozen because of the shock. Behind me, my husband was scanning the room and taking it all in with disbelief.

I went to lay my head next to my mother and told her how much I loved her and that she was the best mother in the world. I took her rollers out of her hair, and I remembered her hair being soaking wet from the cardiac arrest. If I were to describe what I was going through, I would say it was a depersonalization. I felt like I could see what everyone was doing, including myself, but I was not connected to it.

Chaplain Ed, a dear friend of my mom, walked in and gave a new and fresh hope. He took her hand and said, "Clara, God is able. Just liked He raised Lazarus, He can raise you, too." He summoned her back and told me to put on her favorite music. I did, and we all began to pray because her life depended on it. For a moment, I felt hopeful for a miracle and was thinking, *Yes!*

Why hadn't this occurred to me to pray without ceasing in any and all circumstances? I beat myself up about this for a long time. Maybe you have, too, but in a crisis, it can happen. When you are going through a critical and devastating moment, what you know to do, all of a sudden, you can't even think to do.

Chaplain Ed read scriptures and draped the Bible across her chest, and through his tears, he prayed for what seemed to have been 20 minutes. We watched her attentively, waiting for her to cough or move at any movement. The hope we had eventually faded, and we realized God had chosen to take her home and that she was not coming back.

The news had spread as friends and loved ones were waiting in the lobby, including coworkers and members of her prayer group.

A dear friend who had heard the news, Mrs. Chidi, had come frantically through the waiting room and said, "Damita, where is Clara? Damita, tell me she is okay!" Seeing the look on my face, she screamed, "No! No! Take me to her! I want to see her," she said. She was taken to the room where she prayed and talked for quite a while. Mrs. Chidi and Mom were supposed to meet after church that day; they had been planning this get together for a while.

The time eventually comes when there is nothing else that the medical staff or you can do. It's time to call a funeral home to pick up your loved one. Arrangements have to be made, which is the next dreaded phase. Life can really become a blur at that moment and for the days and weeks to come. I felt a sense of defeat and desertion by leaving my mom there. There is not anything in life that can prepare you for a moment like that.

LIFE LESSONS

1. After losing a loved one, some in the early stages of grief question what could have been done differently to obtain a different outcome. Some blame themselves as they endure guilt, which is not uncommon. Choose to focus on what you have done and stay present to move forward and avoid building a tower of sadness and despair.

2. You can't change what has happened, but you can obtain something from it. A well-known AA saying is this: "God grant me the serenity to accept the things that I cannot change, the courage to change the things that I can and the wisdom to know the difference."

3. Change is a part of life. Change is inevitable. The experience of losing a

loved one can change you and cause you to see and live life differently. Be open to new growth and changes.

4. You have gained and benefitted so much through a life full of experiences with your loved one. The huge loss that you feel is a result of the huge love that you have. Remember your loved one through this lens of love.

EXERCISE

What impact has your loved one made on your life? Write about this in your journal, describing what your loved one meant to you.

7

THE REWIND BUTTON

There will usually be a moment in grieving when you will return in your mind to the last day, the last conversation, and the last experience you had with your loved one. For me, I wondered if she saw that moment coming when she would pass into eternity. Could she have known? Let's process.

About two months before my mom passed, she shared a dream she had. As she usually did, she would track me down and say, "Let me tell you about a dream I had."

In the dream, she was with God and hovering over the earth, and they were dialoging. She said, "Lord, what is this that I see?" She described what she saw as a lot of dead bodies under the ground that she could clearly see. The bodies were scattered and positioned like a crime scene with the yellow tape around the scene.

The Lord replied, "You don't remember our conversation?"

She stated, "What conversation?"

He replied, "The one we had before the foundations of the world and before you were formed in your mother's womb."

She slowly replied, "No, I don't." Then, she woke up.

She told me that she had wanted to go back to sleep and get the rest and get the answers to her questions. She asked me, "What do you think that meant?"

Reflecting back, I wonder if God had given her a glimpse? Did He give me a glimpse? I say that because, sometimes, I would wonder whether I could ever face that day. Seeing my parents ageing and preparing for retirement, I would become sad and have to turn off my thoughts. My mom was always vibrant, energetic, fun, and young at heart. The thought of anything happening to her was unimaginable.

In the dream that Mom shared, I found comfort and the answer to what I thought it meant. To me, it gave a beginning and an end of a story. She had originated with God and was given a purpose, served her purpose, and returned to God with a fulfilled purpose and with a job well done. The dream she shared let me know all was well.

Although I may now have more understanding and insight, that doesn't mean that I escaped anger. Anger is a normal stage of grief, but the goal is not to hold on to anger. In my moment of disconnection, I will admit I was not seeking God and praying like I know I needed to. I felt let down by God and was deeply hurt that He had allowed my mom to go.

In grief, there is a need to blame someone. It could be the person who died, God, others, or even one's self. Anger may be displayed by discontinuing prayer, refusing to attend church or socials, or ceasing to do things that were once meaningful. It as if you don't give yourself permission to indulge or do anything pleasurable because it just doesn't seem desirable. The willingness and motivation are unavailable.

In anger, I can recall saying, "God, my mom loved You, she was a prayer warrior, and healing was her ministry. So why didn't You heal her?"

He didn't answer me right away but later responded, "The answer to your question is I did not heal your mother because your mother was not sick. It was her time to come home, and the life she confessed is the life she lived." I sat in my seat in awe of what I had just heard. That statement that day set me free. There were no more questions. I no longer blamed myself for not seeing it coming or for wondering what else I could have done. God set me free from the frustration of the "what if" path.

Free yourself from blame, let go of anger, and reflect on the loving memories.

LIFE LESSONS

1. As you reflect, let go of anger, blame, and responsibilities for matters that you do not or could not control. Death is something we cannot control. Take hold of what you can control. You can control what you are willing to allow into your life right now, such as the courage to heal.

2. Let the promises of God, His grace, and His love carry you through. Get a scripture to meditate on, and offer up to God the broken pieces of your heart. He is able to mend your broken heart.

3. Don't live in the past because you are still in the present, and your loved ones are in your future. You are still making memories, and believe it or not, good things are still to come.

I will lift up mine eyes unto the hills, from whence cometh my help. My help cometh from the Lord, which made heaven and earth. (Psa. 121:1-2)

Trust in the Lord with all your heart, and do not depend on your own understanding. (Prov. 3:5)

EXERCISE

If you have been experiencing anger (or another negative emotion), visualize yourself placing anger in front of you. View its size and color. Ask yourself how long you plan to allow it to stay. Ask yourself what you are getting from holding onto that anger.

What difficulties has it caused you? What will you decide to do with it?

Breathe in deeply five times in a row, and each time you exhale, think about the anger being released. After completing your breathing exercises, decide if you want to take your anger (or other experienced emotions) back or if you want to leave it on the table and walk away.

Today, choose to let go of your toxic emotions, and walk in peace. Believe what you have just stated because believing it will determine your ability to receive it.

8

GOING THROUGH THE MOTIONS

The first few hours, days, and weeks were a blur. I talked to people and hugged them. I gave remarks at the viewing and assisted others. I realized what was going on, and I was robotically responding. But emotionally, I was not connected. This is sometimes referred to as being "in a fog" in which you can physically see, but it just seems like a blur while you are passing through it. Where were the tears? When were they going to come?

Though, whenever I showered, the tears would flow. I would let the water run for a long time, which seemed to represent the tears I was releasing. When the shower stopped, so did the tears... as if to say, "It's show time." I had to be strong for my dad, my kids, and everyone else. Everyone was watching me and standing by in case I had an emotional breakdown. I wanted to be strong because my family needed me.

In grief, we often put on a face that others want to see but does not often reflect what we truly feel. Why do we make "our" grief about others? Why do we feel that being vulnerable and crying are signs of weakness? It takes a strong person to be in touch with his or her feelings. Be true to yourself. Be true to what you feel because you can't heal what you don't feel.

The journey begins with recognizing, accepting, and allowing your feelings to be expressed because this is a vital step in recovering effectively.

LIFE LESSONS

1. Be true to yourself and to what you feel is real.
2. Your grief is all about you. It is your grief, and you define it.

3. Remove your expectations of others. Accept them for who they are and where they are.

4. Take moments alone to process your feelings.

EXERCISE

Sit in a quiet space on the floor with your legs crossed, yoga style, or in a chair in which you can stretch out and totally relax. As your arms are draped across your legs in the yoga position or hanging over your chair, capture everything that you have been emotionally carrying. Allow your thoughts to roll down your arms, down to your fingertips, and then drip off.

After the last thought drips, take four or five deep breaths until you begin to feel lighter.

Next, take time to center and imagine a spotlight. Pick up your emotions that dripped off onto the floor under the spotlight. Examine your feelings. Have you expressed them before and, if so, how? Where were they located in your body? [e.g. your head (headache), neck/shoulders (pain), stomach (digestive problems), or other places throughout the body]? Take the time to locate where your emotions were housed and confirm that those areas are now free and clear.

9

No Time to Feel

Initially, I felt that, if I slowed down, the world would just sit on top of me. I felt that, if I stopped to be emotional, those emotions would overwhelm me and cause me to lose control. My mother's passing was something that caught me off guard and that I had no control over. The one thing I thought I had control over was my feelings.

On the opposite end, my father was a constant flowing river of tears. It would hurt me so much to see his pain; however, I knew it was necessary. I had never seen that amount of pain expressed by my dad. I felt helpless at times. In some instances, he would close himself off and not want to have anyone around when he was hurting, even me. I worried about him all the time and prayed, "Lord, what can I do to help him?" The simplest answer came, which was that I just needed to be there.

When we are around those who are grieving, we sometimes don't know what to say or do. Often, the awkwardness comes through, and being there seems like not enough, yet it says so much.

In the past, it bothered me to hear people say, "I am sorry for your loss." I vowed to never say, "I am sorry for your loss" because choose to think of how much was gained and how much richer my life is because of my mom. Also, I didn't lose my mom. I know where she is, and I will always have her in my heart and memories. That may sound petty, but for me, it was real.

You may also find yourself intolerant of things and super sensitive and reactive about conversations that you have with others while you are grieving. You may find that you're more sensitive to certain words. There may be high irritability and minimum tolerance as your emotions are under transition. Your reactivity to things may be elevated.

Attempting to be there for my dad to assist him—as well as my family—in getting through my mom's passing felt like I was putting what I was feeling on a shelf. I planned to get to my feelings when I could, but I often discovered there was no time. In some ways, I believe I distracted myself by my involvement in my family's recovery to avoid my own because it was too painful. Also, I just didn't know where to begin.

One day, I began to journal and write a letter as I often advise others to do. After writing a page, I felt numb and realized it was pointless. My emotions were still suppressed, and writing was not appearing to have the cathartic effect intended. It is interesting how we can hurt so much on the inside, yet nothing gets released on the outside.

To this day, I have not attempted that exercise again because I still have not felt able to emotionally connect to the devastation that I have experienced. When I try to have a moment to release my feelings, I hear my mom's voice saying, "No…

No… We are not having that." So my feelings are still on a shelf, and maybe yours are as well. Perhaps you feel like you are functional and want to leave well enough alone, but usually, everything on the shelf has an expiration. The time will come. The time needs to come. And I will embrace the time when it does.

LIFE LESSONS

1. Accept that you can't heal and take care of yourself while accommodating and helping others through the grieving process at the same time.
2. Don't be afraid to seek counseling. Talking is like medicine for the soul.
3. Consider a grief group so you won't feel alone on this journey.
4. Establish boundaries for yourself in the healing process.

EXERCISES

1. Get a journal, and write letters. If
   you are emotionally blocked, try
   again later. Writing a letter to your
   deceased loved one can be very cathartic. Consider using a picture col-
   lage or a video that can help you to
   focus during those times of reflec-
   tion.

2. Get a memorable quilt made so that,
   during your time to cuddle with a
   book, you can feel close and a sense
   connection with your deceased loved
   one. Quilts can be made to include
   clothing fabric of your loved one's favorite shirt or pajamas, for example.

3. If you are used to sleeping you're
   your loved one, try using a body pillow. Hold/hug the pillow, close your
   eyes, and welcome your thoughts

about your loved one. Feel free to speak them out loud.

4. Exercise and work on breathing five deep breaths, exhaling and inhaling throughout your day.

5. Listen to soothing soundscape music, jazz, or soaking music to relax and reflect. This is a good way to thaw out emotionally.

10

HERE COMES THE RAIN

At the time of writing this chapter, I am almost eight months along in my journey, and I can tell you the rain is coming. The rain represents that emotional release that may not come in a big flood but in sporadic rain showers. Rain is rain in whatever way it comes because people process and grieve differently. There is not a certain formula for grief; it is independently formulated. That is why, in this book, I am not trying to tell you how to grieve. You need to establish and personalize it to fit you; however, I am emphasizing the importance of taking time to grieve because it is necessary and healthy. In sharing my journey personally as well as professionally, my aim is to open up some thoughts for you to explore and to help you start a conversation to process your grief.

How will you know if you have properly grieved a loss? My first response would be that you would know. I realize that this response may not be helpful or answer your question. Properly grieving a loss means that you permit time to allow painful thoughts and feelings to surface and allow yourself to feel your grief and express it however necessary. It is a process and happens through a series over time, but in time, you can get to a point where you think about or talk about the memories with less pain and difficulty.

I would have never thought I would be writing a book on grief and certainly not my journey of recovering from grief; however, upon God's nudging, it began. During the writing of this book, my tears have flowed, and the rain has come. I have come to realize that, through writing to help others, I also have been healing. What an amazing God we serve. He found a unique way to release me from my emotional burden.

LIFE LESSONS

1. Let it rain. Let it rain. Cry yourself a river. It is okay.
2. Honor your true feelings and listen to your heart calling out to you.
3. Tears can take us deeper than our words ever can. Talk from your heart today.
4. Tears have power to heal physically and psychologically. Tears are healthy and good for you. And when your loved one died, it felt like a portion of you died, too. But also, a part of your loved one lives on in you as well.

EXERCISE

Get some quiet time in which you can be still, emotionally and physically. No movements and no distractions. Place your loved one's picture in front of you. Focus in, and think about him or her. What did he or she mean to you? How do you feel about him or her? Capture what you miss about your loved one, take a deep breath, exhale, and feel it. Remember your loved one's touch, scent, and unique things about him or her. Take some time to get there, and when you are there, center your thoughts on your loved one, allowing your emotions to rise within. Then, exhale your emotions. Repeat this process several times until you begin to *feel* a release and get your breakthrough.

11

SPIRITUAL AVOIDANCE

Praying without ceasing is what we should do, but it is not always what we do. I didn't pray for a long time after my mother passed. I knew I needed to, and I knew prayers would help. At the same time, it was too painful.

My mom spent lots of time in prayer. We prayed together. She believed in and taught me the power of prayer, but I just couldn't. Instead, I prayed surface prayers that I am sure didn't move God or me. Was I angry with God? Did I feel let down by God?

Perhaps you have been avoiding Him as well. This is not good, but it is normal and understandable in grief. Confessing this is the beginning of healing. It is normal to feel disappointment as tragedy has happened despite that you have believed, prayed, cried out to God, and stood on His Word. You feel angry, let down, and forsaken. Jesus felt that way on the cross and cried out, "My God, my God, why have you forsaken me?" (Matt. 27:46; Mark 15:34) It happens, but quickly, we need to redirect our emotions so they can work in a favorable way for us.

Even in our pain, God is there the whole time to hold us, to wipe our tears away, and to comfort us with His love. He assures us that we are going to be okay despite how much we are hurting. Spiritual avoidance keeps us off track and going nowhere or in the wrong direction. When we are avoiding God spiritually, we usually are angry or not wanting to move from what we feel. Or, are we not wanting to feel at all? We may be so emotionally flat-lined that the only energy and strength that we have is to say "Jesus."

When I finally began to pray effectively and fervently, God moved and began to heal my shattered heart.

LIFE LESSONS

1. Find comfort in reading the Bible to know God's promises.
2. Prayer reveals the answers to the questions you have; don't hesitate to ask.
3. God is for us in both good times and bad. He is your friend during your time of need.

EXERCISE

Set aside a time daily for you to exercise spiritually so you can get back into shape. For this exercise, I recommend that you get a Bible, a devotional book (*Jesus Calling* and *Jesus Today* by Sarah Young are ones I would recommend), a journal book, a tissue, and a pen. Set aside 15-20 minutes a day to journal your feelings, thoughts, and requests. Read a scripture verse and apply it to your journey and pray. A devotional song can be helpful as well to get in tune spiritually.

12

KEEPSAKES

In the beginning, you may find yourself surrounded by pictures, clothing, and other items that belonged to your loved one. That's all you have tangibly to hold onto. These things can provide a sense of comfort and feeling of connection. Initially, I surrounded myself with pictures of my mom, I wore something of hers, and I viewed videos of her to hear her voice. These things were like a security blanket for me. For the first several months, I proudly wore something of my mom's every day, whether jewelry or clothing. It was my way to feel close to her.

Have you noticed that, when people's loved ones pass away, they get t-shirts, paraphernalia, videos, and other things made to remember their loved one? They don't want to lose one thought or memory. They want to hold on tight and never forget. They want to feel a sense of having their loved one with them.

When I would make my dad's bed, I would spray my mom's perfume on his pillow. He kept a large picture of her on the nightstand. Often, he would just talk out loud to her as his way to heal. This is similar to what we call the "empty chair" in counseling. We have a picture of the deceased in front of the person and ask him or her to talk as if that loved one was present. This is a valuable therapeutic technique. We also encourage the grieving person to write a letter to the deceased loved one in which his or her feelings can be released.

Sometimes, people cannot release their loved one's belongings for months or even years. You don't have to release them in a set period of time. You have to go with what is comfortable for you. Again, there is no right answer. Holding on physically is tied to holding on emotionally. When you begin to heal, you can release the things because you realize it is not the things that keep your loved one close; it is the memories and the love that keep them with you, and these intangibles are always accessible.

When you change the room around and release things, it can represent a helpful change for you, which will encourage you to keep it moving and to realize that change is okay. This will move you closer to acceptance in grief. Acceptance is part of healing.

LIFE LESSONS

1. Releasing does not leave you without or empty.
2. Change is necessary in the process of healthy grieving.
3. Moving forward is not forgetting but learning to live life differently.
4. Your loved one left a deposit and investment with you that continues to appreciate with time.

EXERCISE

In your journal, think about what you are holding on to. Is it physical or emotional? What do you think would happen if you let it go?

If you have children, you watch them grow and let them go. They leave, but even though you may not see them as you had before, letting them go is a process in their growth and yours.

In order to grow, you have to release. What do you need to release so you can grow?

13

TWO AT ONCE

When my mom passed, I felt as if my father went, too. He seemed lost and without hope. He would call and cry nearly every day, it seemed, which would hurt and leave me feeling lost. He was my hero and someone I could always go to and feel protected by.

One morning at 5:00 a.m., he left the following message for me: "Today is the sixth, and it makes six months since your mom left. I wish it were *me*." Other calls would allude to the same feelings, and suddenly, I felt alone and abandoned by both of my parents. I was angry that he couldn't help me, be there for me, and soothe my fears as the only parent I had left. He couldn't, and I had to realize that his world was shattered and that he couldn't be the dad I once knew or needed at that time. I had to accept his grief.

My husband did a great job of being there for me and, often, just held me as I cried myself to sleep. He assured me that I was not alone. I found comfort in my husband, kids, and friends who supported me.

When you are grieving, it is easy to isolate and withdraw; however, allow the support and love of others. Sometimes, you may feel that you just want to be alone. Sometimes, that is needed. However, grief is a lonely path, so why be alone and lonely? Allow others to be there with you and for you; this will help with your recovery. You may not know what you need or make the best decisions when you are grieving, so allowing others to care for you during time of bereavement is beneficial.

When you are the grieving child as I was, and the living parent "needs" you, you have to balance your time. My dad needed me, and I needed him. We realized that it was hard to meet each other's needs at that time. I can say that, three years later, my dad is on his way back, emotionally and physically, and I am grateful. I have my dad again! Healing takes time. Don't give up if you feel that you have experienced a similar situation.

I can't imagine, but it would be a similar situation if a parent lost a child and still had a household to run and other children who needed him or her despite the loss of the child. Balancing time for others and time for one's self is critically important, and equal distribution is required. Also, recognize that you sometimes need time to replenish because you don't have anything left to give.

LIFE LESSONS

1. Allow the support of others when grieving. Be honest about what you need because others don't always know. Help others know how to help you.

2. Balance time for yourself on the path to healing.

3. Protect yourself emotionally during this time. Don't allow others to add additional stress to your life.

4. Avoid expecting something from others that they cannot give. This will only lead to further disappointment.

EXERCISE

In your journal, write about the difficulties you are experiencing. What decisions can you make to reduce the difficulties? Include how you can begin to apply self-care.

14

FILLING MY TANK

Although I cannot see or touch my mom, I can feel her presence. I knew her so well. She was my best friend, and I can still hear her as if she were speaking today. The love she provided was so unbelievable that, even in her absence, there is still abundance. That abundance will carry me until we meet again.

As I came home from the hospital on that unforgettable day, I sat in my prayer room. What is a prayer room? My prayer room is where I spend time with God and seek Him on a daily basis. It is where I get revelation, inspiration, ideas, and answers to my prayers. I spend time with God in my secret place so I can be alone with Him and get answers to my prayers and requests. That morning, I felt poured into by God. I felt strengthened almost immediately, and as I looked in the mirror, I heard my mom's voice in my heart saying,

> I know you will be sad, but I am not gone. I am right here with you. Every time you look in the mirror and see yourself, you will see me.

I wiped away my tears, and a great sense of peace came over me. Ever since then, my head has been up and not down. I am looking and moving forward because she is ahead of me and not behind me.

I encourage you to find your special room or another place where you can spend time with your thoughts and memories. You may hear from your heart and be comforted by your cherished memories. Anytime you get low emotionally, you can go to the archives of your memory and have a moment. Perhaps you will discover that your tank is filling up like mine and that you don't have to run on empty.

LIFE LESSONS

1. Memories never expire and can be activated anytime.
2. You have a tankful of love that will never run out. Activate your tank by spending time reflecting on some of your fond memories.
3. Love never reduces its value. Hold on to your valuables. They are worth something.

EXERCISE

Write down statements that your loved one used to say and conversations the two of you had together. You may even want to write them in red so they will stand out. Fill your tank with things they would say to you right now. Refer back to this section whenever you need encouragement or an emotional hug.

15

I Am Living Again

Each day, I feel stronger, more hopeful, and more encouraged. It has now been over two years since I started this journey. I pray that this book is helping you to either begin this journey or to get unstuck along the path to feel hopeful, strong, and encouraged again. Finishing this book has brought closure for me and has helped me to move from pain to purpose.

After giving myself a year to process my grief, unbelievably, the first grief case I received as a counselor was a young lady who had just lost her mom. I remember saying, "God, I am not ready for this."

In reply, I heard, "You can do this. You understand." With a heighted sensitivity to grief and loss like never before, I was committed and ready to support and assist in her recovery process.

If you have been there, you know, and you can speak of that hurt in a way that shows you care and understand. The empathy you have will lead you right into the heart of someone going through the challenge of grief and loss.

Writing this book has been cathartic for me. It has been a way to share my journey and provide insight regarding emotional detours that you may encounter, how to yield and proceed with caution, and how to stop and make turns periodically.

Turning my pain into purpose inspired me to start a greeting card company, Heaven Sent Greeting Cards, and to write this book. My cousin, Marilyn Harvey, joined me in the greeting card company, and today, we actively share the passion of creating cards that comfort hurting hearts in a unique way. In addition, we have specialty cards for every occasion. Big or small, we have thought of it all.

Consider turning your own pain into purpose. It can really be a blessing.

LIFE LESSONS

1. Grief is an indicator of love. Because of love, we experience grief. We would prefer to have loved and grieve than never to have enjoyed our precious loved ones.
2. Life will never go back to what it was, but it will be okay.
3. Don't be afraid to live life again although it will be a new normal.

EXERCISE

Try doing something that you have given up or avoided since your loss. Include a friend for support, if needed. Explore what feelings you are experiencing. You may have to repeat efforts before you can begin to feel more comfortable. Give yourself permission to enjoy it. Don't be discouraged, and don't give up. It gets easier with time. Be encouraged.

16

THE FIRST HOLIDAYS

Life can feel like a roller coaster full of ups and downs. A few months may go by with you feeling okay. In the weeks thereafter, it may feel impossible. It is then you may think, *I thought I was doing better*. You very well may be doing better. It's not necessarily a setback but part of the road to recovery.

The first holidays are difficult to get through, and some opt to avoid them altogether. You can participate at whatever level you feel comfortable.

For me, it has been helpful to keep some of my old traditions as well as add some new ones. Instead of having celebration dinners at mom's house, they are now at my house. I change some of the dishes but keep our favorites. We are even adding another family vacation during the Christmas time to change the location and the feel of things. Again, however, you will need to consider what works for you so that it will be conducive.

With family and friends, you shouldn't have to mask your emotions. They understand and, perhaps, feel the pain as well. When you need a moment of privacy, take it as often as needed. You can be creative with how you choose to remember and honor your loved one on that day through apparel, a lit candle by your loved one's picture, talking about memories from last year's holiday, or by doing nothing at all. Remember that you are the designer.

For birthdays and anniversaries, you could prepare a special dinner at home or go out for dinner or lunch with the company of family and/or friends. You could choose to have your loved one's favorite entrée or dessert.

My mother enjoyed desserts, especially if it was chocolate. Every birthday, I have a "Clara's Chocolate Day" to honor her on her birthday with friends and family. We all participate and post pictures on Facebook. It really helps to absorb the emotional heaviness of the day.

Consider if you would like to celebrate the memory of your loved one on holidays and special occasions. The *how* is up to you. Here are a few ideas:

- Plan and prepare ahead for how you would like to spend your holiday or special occasion. It can take away some of the anxiety and give you something to look forward to.
- If you have spearheaded events in the past, it may be a good idea for you to relinquish the responsibilities for the first year. I am sure your friends and family will understand.
- Surround yourself with people who love and support you.
- Draw comfort from others.

- Ask each person to say something he/she remembers about your loved one.
- Meet at the cemetery and release balloons or place flowers.
- Ask each person to make a dessert that reminds them of your loved one, and have them give the dessert a name in honor of your loved one.
- Ask each person to light a candle and say something about your loved one that was special.
- Have special place settings.
- Create an online tribute.
- Create ornaments.
- Collect money in your loved one's name and give it to a charity.
- Go to a paint night to celebrate your loved one.

If you decide to keep holidays and special occasions low key, that is okay as well. There is no right or wrong answer. What matters is what feels right for you. The goal is to move through the holidays and special occasions by effective means that will help you cope well.

17

UNTIL WE MEET AGAIN

"Until we meet again" is a phrase that we often hear. What special meaning does it have for you? To me, this means that I will continue the work that I was doing before, but now, I will do it even better. In addition, I feel like a baton has been passed to continue some of the things that were near and dear to my mom. I consider "until we meet again" to be a time to honor my mom and experience another depth of love for her.

Every day and in unique ways, I continue to discover how special and unique my mom was. She was that special kind of person who would encourage you and only see what you *could* do rather than focusing on what you *couldn't* do. She was full of life and fun to be around. She would give you those spiritual nuggets that would make you think hard and task you to read books or scriptures, to sing a song, or to complete a spiritual assignment… all to develop the gifts and the spiritual leader within you. She would pray with people at any given time, and it didn't matter if you had time or not because prayer time was vital, and she never missed a moment to pray. She would share revelations that she would receive and share insights with those who would listen. She was always ready to talk about God, and that I will truly miss.

As a mother and a friend, she was absolutely the best! I never saw her angry or say anything unkind. She was always an example and a teacher who I learned so much from, and she influenced me greatly. The mother, wife, and professional I am today is a result of her. If I had to give one word that described her, it would be *love*.

Her love never failed me in any situation, not even this one. Although I initially felt angry because she left me after saying she would never leave me, I realized that she never really left my heart. I still feel her love, and I now know the incredible power of a mother's love. It is like no other. Whether it is a mother-child relationship or otherwise, believe in the power of love. It never fails.

This book and journey has afforded me an opportunity to accept my new normal and find my own creative way to meet each day with new hope and enthusiasm to keep her memory and her accomplishments alive now and for generations to come… until we meet again.

LIFE LESSONS

1. Love never fails, and love never ends.
2. Recognize the power of your love, and embrace it.
3. Love will see you through, even in these times.

EXERCISE

Write about *who* your loved one was to you. Describe the relationship and your love for that person. What can you do in the memory of your loved one to honor him or her? What better time to do it than now?

18

YOUR PRAYER

There is incredible power in prayer. Tap into the power of prayer by creating your own prayer for this season of your life. Pour out your heart, and tell God what you feel. If you have been angry and carrying unforgiveness in your heart, lay that at His feet in your prayer. What's on your heart?

(Below is an outline to include that may find helpful. At the end of this section, write and then say your prayer out loud.)

PRAY FOR COMFORT

> The Lord is close to the broken hearted; he rescues those whose spirits are crushed. (Psa. 34:18)

> Blessed are those who mourn, for they shall be comforted. (Matt. 5:4)

> I will turn their mourning into gladness. I will give them comfort and joy instead of sorrow. (Jer. 31:13)

PRAY FOR HEALING

> For the Lord hath comforted His people, and will have mercy on the afflicted. (Isa. 49:13b)

> He heals the broken hearted and binds up their wounds. (Psa. 147:3)

PRAY FOR PEACE

> I am leaving you with a gift—peace of mind and heart! And the peace I give is not fragile like the peace the world gives. So don't be troubled or afraid. (John 14:27)

Please write your prayer in the space below...

19

A Prayer for You

Dear God, I want to lift up your dear children to you who are grieving the loss of their loved ones. Their hearts are broken, Father, and are in need of mending.

Please, touch them with Your unfailing love and fill their hearts with the strength and courage to heal. Let Your Word bring comfort to them and give hope. May your love lighten this dark place that they are in so they can see past today and into a brighter tomorrow. Let them feel your presence so they will know that you are with them and that they are not alone.

May they find some comfort in knowing that their loved ones are safe and protected in your care. Lord, may You fill their lonely nights and difficult days. Allow them to understand that their pain is

Your pain and that You are unable to rest until those who mourn are comforted. From Heaven, let your peace fall and surround them right now. Saturate them with Your love, hold them close, and don't let go until they can find strength again.

Thank You, Lord, for your unfailing love and for answering. In the name of Jesus, Amen.

FINAL WORDS

I wish you peace and comfort on this journey. I hope this book has been encouraging and has provided some tools for you to use on the road to healing. Be encouraged as you go forward, no matter what you may encounter along the way. You can't control what's to come, but you can manage your reaction to it. People are people and may have expectations regarding how long you should grieve. It can be overwhelming to get advice about your grief from others, and you may have to establish boundaries.

How you grieve is important. Healing from grief is a gradual process, and there is no specific timetable. Some people can feel better in shorter periods of time while it can take much longer for others... even years. However, the goal is to keep moving forward.

Be patient with yourself, and require patience from others as well. Allow grief to unfold naturally. Grieving is a process that takes time.

CPSIA information can be obtained
at www.ICGtesting.com
Printed in the USA
FFOW02n0138291116
29716FF